D1545521

Don't Let Go Of Your
DREAMS

DON'T LET GO OF YOUR DREAMS

ISBN 0 - 88144 - 171 - 6
Unless otherwise stated, all Scripture quotations are taken
from *The King James Version* of the Bible.

Jerry Savelle Ministries
P.O. Box 748
Crowley, TX 76036

JERRY SAVELLE

Don't Let Go Of Your DREAMS

**Once God has planted a
dream within your heart,
He has every intention
of bringing it to pass.**

CONTENTS

Chapter
1

Catch The Spirit Of Revival

Don't ever lose your dreams! I don't care if it looks like they are never going to come to pass! I would rather keep dreaming and it never come to pass, and yet know that I have drive and motivation in my life and a reason for existence, than have no dream at all!

People who have no purpose in life are miserable people. Have you ever seen people who have no goals, no dreams, no vision, and no purpose? They're miserable! I don't enjoy being around them. I want to help them and minister to them, but I don't "pal around" with people like that. They'll pull you down to their level, and if you're not careful, you wind up just like them with "no reason to live".

Jesus has a purpose for your life! YOU have a dream or a destiny that God has given you, and you are expected to hold on to it! Don't give up - even if it looks like your dreams are so far out of reach that there is no way they could ever come to pass.

God is not finished with you yet! Maybe we should all wear a sign around our neck that says "Under Construction!"

Acts 26:16 says, "But rise, and stand upon thy feet: for I have appeared unto thee for this PURPOSE, to make thee a minister and a witness both of these things which thou hast seen, and of those things in the which I will appear unto thee."

When God gives you purpose, then He is also the one who will make it come to pass. Your responsibility is to hold on to the dreams!

Even if you have blown it and made mistakes, had setbacks spiritually, and even let sin back into your life, (that is not a license to continue doing it) but you must remember that God is a God of restoration.

Acts 3:19 says, "Repent ye therefore, and be converted, that your sins may be blotted out, when the times of refreshing shall come from the presence of the Lord." God wants to give us a time of refreshing. That's what the "spirit of revival" is - a time of refreshing, recovering from the effects of heat, and recapturing your divine destiny!

How do you "catch the spirit of revival"? The Bible says that "in His presence is fullness of joy". First, you need to go before God and repent that your sins may be blotted out! Second, you need to spend time in fellowship and prayer with the Father. Spending time with the Lord will produce joy on the inside of you, and that joy will give you the strength you need to get back on your feet and go after the calling God has put on your life! Nehemiah 8:10 says, "for the joy of the Lord is your strength".

Determine now to place yourself in this position: as you spend time in the presence of the Lord, you will be full of His joy, if you are full of His joy, you will have the strength of God in your life, with His strength, you WILL be able to accomplish His purpose and calling for your life. On the other hand, if you are not spending time with God, you won't have any joy, if you don't have any joy, you won't have any strength, and if you don't have any strength, you will never fulfill your purpose and dreams!

That is why it is so important to catch the spirit of revival in your life again - God wants to restore that JOY in your life! In other words, revival restores JOY! Revival restores HOPE for the future! Revival restores the excitement in waiting for your dream and watching it come to pass! God wants you to have that joy back in your life!

The spirit of revival will produce a force within you which will cause you to be DETERMINED to fulfill your purpose and dreams! Spend time with God and get "revival" in your life!

Chapter
2

Are You On Fire?

Fire is a consuming force that when ignited, it will intensify and grow. As we allow God to ignite within us His vision, purpose, and dreams for our life, it will begin to intensify and grow until it completely consumes our very being.

As with fire, your dream needs ignition and fuel to burn. God will ignite a dream in your heart, but YOU must continually add the fuel of the Word of God to your dream in order to keep it burning. There will be opportunities for other people, the enemy, and even yourself to try to throw water on your dreams, but you must continually protect and feed your dream until it comes to pass. Be determined NOW to let that fire motivate you, drive you and consume you to keep your dreams alive!

Proverbs 29:18 says, "Where there is no vision, the people perish." People without a vision are nonproductive people! There is nothing more tragic than to let go of your vision and have no drive, no motivation and no fire!

You can get around certain people and know in five minutes - they have no vision! Why? They have no fire! They have no drive! No motivation! They are just - existing! Their favorite scripture is "Come quickly, Lord Jesus!" They just want out!

When you spend time in God's Word and realize that God has called YOU for a purpose, there is a zeal or a fire that burns on the inside of you. Just knowing that God thinks so much of you that He called YOU to fulfill this calling should excite you!

Some people have the attitude of "well, I've tried this or that and nothing happened". That's not an excuse to give up!

The Bible says that FAITH comes by hearing and hearing by the Word of God. We need to constantly refresh ourselves in the scriptures (add fuel to the fire). Go out of your way to spend time with the Lord and read His Word. You have to stir yourself up in the Word.

It is very easy to become relaxed and not go after anything, but you have to hunger for more of God's Word and hunger for your dreams to be fulfilled. Don't just settle for a life with no purpose! God wants to use YOU! Will you let Him?

God responds to hunger. He wants you to hunger and thirst for this vision. Don't just say, "if it happens, it happens". Go after it! Jesus said, "When you are hungry and thirsty, you shall be filled." Don't wait any longer! God is waiting on you to get that fire back in your life and hunger to see this dream fulfilled!

Chapter
3

Be

Aggressive!

Aggressive does not mean obnoxious. It simply means you are energetic in pursuing particular goals. The word aggressive implies that an individual would be marked by a driving forceful energy or initiative.

We must be aggressive in our faith and actions to see God's purpose and dreams for our life fulfilled. It will take the forceful energy of the Holy Spirit on the inside of us, our own initiative, and an energetic attitude in pursuing our dreams to see them come to pass. Aggressive people never give up because of outside hindrances or attacks!

Have you experienced the attacks of the devil? We all have. When you are under the effects of heat and pressure, the devil aims his attacks at getting you to lose your sense of direction and purpose.

He will try everything to get you to GIVE UP! Satan does not want you to fulfill your divine destiny.

On the other hand, the Bible shares HOPE for the future. No matter what you are going through or what obstacle may be before you, HOPE will keep you at rest, firm and steady, when your mind is being bombarded with thoughts of giving up!

The Bible paints images on the inside of your heart of who you are, what you are, and what you are entitled to possess as a child of the living God. That revelation knowledge from the Word gives you vision, dreams and goals, and when you know that God has given you purpose, it causes zeal to rise up on the inside of you, and you become AGGRESSIVE!

After realizing what rightfully belongs to you, you can never again be passive about your dreams, you have to be aggressive and go after what God has called you to do.

Once you find out that you have authority in the Name of Jesus, you can't be passive about that anymore. Once you find out that by His stripes you are healed, you can't be passive about sickness anymore. You attack that sickness with the Word of God! Once you find out that God has a PURPOSE for your life, you go after it! You have to fulfill what God has called YOU to do.

Even though it may appear that your dream may never come to pass or it may not be the "thing to do" anymore - you better do what God told YOU to do! Success is fulfilling what God told YOU to do, not what God told someone else to do!

There are many people who have dreams for their life, but why is it that so many never see them come to pass? The fulfillment or the failure of your dreams is determined by your attitude. Fulfillment comes by an aggressive attitude; whereas, failure is the result of a passive attitude.

There are three types of people: people who make things happen (Aggressive); people who hope things might happen (Passive); and people who wonder "what happened?" (Wonderers). YOU be the one who makes things happen!

Since you became a Believer, I am sure that God has given you some dreams. There have probably been some dreams that you have followed through with, and some of which you have let go. I challenge you to give some thought to the dreams God has given you. Write them down, aggressively pursue their fulfillment, and check them off as they come to pass! Don't just settle for a life with no purpose! BE AGGRESSIVE!

Chapter
4

*God Does
Not Abort
Dreams*

A dream is a seed that God plants in the fertile soil of your heart. In order for a seed to produce fruit, it must go through a process of development. The first stage is conception. Conception is when God places a vision or a dream in your heart. Once the dream is in your heart, it must go through the second stage, development, before you can give birth to the fulfillment. From the time of conception until the time of fulfillment is the most important time to protect your dream. This is the time when the enemy, other people, and even you may try to abort your dream through unbelief, discouragement, and impatience.

Once God has planted a dream within your heart, He has every intention of bringing it to pass. 1 Thessalonians 5:24

says, "faithful is He who called you, and He also will bring it to pass". As with a baby in the womb of the mother, your dream must be nurtured, cared for, and protected against the forces that would try to abort it.

God gave Abraham a dream: He would be the father of many nations. Even though in the natural, it was impossible to see it come to pass, Abraham believed. He did not abort his dream. Romans 4:16-22 talks of the fulfillment of Abraham's dream. Verses 20 - 21 say, "...with respect to the promise of God (dream), he did not waver in unbelief but grew strong in faith, giving glory to God, (21) and being fully assured that what He had promised, He was able also to perform." This is the type of faith that will cause the dream God has given you to come to pass.

There have been some dreams in my life that I have lost. I have never been to the place where I wanted to quit - that's not an alternative to me, but there have been some times that I have had to go before God and recapture my dream and not let it die.

Sometimes we get so excited about our dreams, and we tell everyone about it and how we are going to do it; we pray about it, we sow seed for it and THEN the first obstacle comes along, and we say "forget it!"

The Lord shared with me one time, "you've planted seed, and you've let weeds grow up around it, but the seed is still in the ground, it's still there - I DO NOT ABORT SEEDS! You planted that seed, and My Word says that your labor is not in vain," He said, "I keep record, and there's still seed in the ground that you are entitled to harvest, and if you'll recapture it, I'll bring it in!" Praise God!

So - don't give up! If you have planted seed for this dream God gave you, it's still in the ground. IT'S STILL THERE! Just start pulling the weeds up around it, and begin watering that seed. Start speaking the Word over your destiny, begin calling those things that are not as though they are, confess scriptures over your life, and pray in the Holy Spirit. Think about it, talk about it, pray about it, and sow seed for it.

It's time for the harvest of your dreams to be fulfilled! Start naming your seed to "recapture your dreams". Water that seed with the Word of God. Then, watch it come to pass!

Chapter
5

Grip It Tightly!

Hebrews 10:23 says, "Let us hold fast the profession of our faith without wavering." Do you know what "hold fast" means? It is a word that we have heard so many times and may not realize the impact it has. Hold fast is taken from the Greek word "katecho". Katecho is a compound of two words: Kata and Echo.

Kata carries the idea of something that comes downward with force. While Echo is defined as "I have" and carries the idea of "I possess". The two words combined together mean not only to embrace something, but to hold it tightly and with force! In other words, to hold fast is to have a firm grip. You take hold of this dream with force, pull it downward and to you, and don't let ANYTHING take it from you!

The devil will try to come in and steal this dream from you, but when you are holding fast to this dream, it becomes a tug-of-war. You must realize that the Holy Ghost is with you, and He will empower you and strengthen you because greater is He that is in you, than he that is in the world! The devil cannot get your dream!

There are two very important factors that the devil will try to use to get you to let go of your dream:

1. TIME. Time has a way of saying, "it's been two years now! Where's your dream?" Long periods of time where it looks like nothing has happened will try to influence you to just go ahead and give up. "If it hasn't happened by now, it never will!" "I'm getting older." DON'T LET GO! God called YOU to fulfill this dream, and He is expecting YOU to carry it out!

2. PEOPLE. There are people that Satan uses from time to time to try to discourage you. They may say, "I thought you were going to do this or that, what happened?" HOLD ON TO IT! "Do you know how much it will cost to do something like that?" HOLD ON TO IT! Don't let the devil use people to distract you from your dreams. Keep your eyes focused on God and keep your heart full of God's Word. He has all the answers to all your questions, and you can do ALL things through Christ who strengthens you. (Philippians 4:13)

Hold fast to this dream and don't let the devil use time or people to steal it from you. If you let up just a little bit, Satan interprets that as SURRENDER! You must hold it tight! Embrace it with force!

Have you ever seen a child that is about to get a spanking? He grabs the door and Mama says, "come in here, you are going to get a whipping!" He has got a hold of the door knob or a hold of the bed, and she's pulling his leg, but he's "holding fast" - he's not going to let go!

We have heard this so many times "hold fast to your confession..." and if we are not careful, we begin to think, "I've done that, what else? Give me a new revelation. Give me something that works!"

Well, if you hold fast, you will not need anything else because holding fast without wavering will cause it to come to pass. God says, "I am faithful who promised." If you hold fast, God will be faithful to bring it to pass!

The attitude we ought to have about our dream is: we seek it, we live for it, we hold fast to it, and God says there will come a time when we will finally SEIZE IT! The object of your dreams has finally come into your embrace and you can say, "It's mine! No one can take it from me!"

Chapter
6

You Have
What
It Takes!

As I was reading the book of Exodus, the Lord had me to study the example of God calling Moses to lead His people out of Egypt. I really began to notice the drastic change that took place in Moses' life throughout the book. Then, I realized that the change came about due to Moses "recapturing" the dreams God gave him. It's obvious at the beginning that Moses was just existing, but when God gave him PURPOSE, and FIRE in his heart to fulfill this purpose, he became a new person.

In the natural, Moses could not have done the things he did, but God supernaturally gave him the qualities he needed to fulfill this vision. Moses began to holdfast to this dream, gripping it tightly with force, and NOTHING and NOBODY could take it away from him. The devil threw all kinds of obstacles his way, and most people would have quit at the first hit, but Moses held fast!   He knew that if he would not let up, just continue embracing this dream, that finally there WOULD come a time when he would SEIZE IT!

From reading the book of Exodus, the Lord showed me seven qualities that will be produced in your life once you have recaptured your vision:

1.   IDENTITY. Vision establishes your identity. God is saying to Moses in Exodus 3:10, (Amplified) "Come now therefore, and I will send you to Pharaoh, that you may bring forth My people, the Israelites, out of Egypt."   God is telling Moses that He has called HIM to confront Pharaoh and lead the people out of Egypt. Moses responds with, "..Who am I, that I should go to Pharaoh and bring the Israelites out of Egypt?"

He's asking for identity. "Who am I that you should call to do this?" God wanted Moses, first of all, to be established in his own identity in God. It's not so much who you are, it's who God is. When you recapture your dreams, it establishes your identity in God.

2. AUTHORITY. Vision establishes authority. In Exodus 3:13, Moses is saying to God, "Behold, when I come to the Israelites and say to them, The God of your fathers has sent me to you, and they say to me, What is His name? What shall I say to them?" And God said, "I AM THAT I AM.." In other words, "you tell them that the 'I Am that I Am' sent you!"

So - vision establishes authority. The authority to walk in that vision. The authority to believe for it to come to pass. Some people may question your authority to do this, but your authority is in the I AM!

3.   CREDIBILITY.   Vision estab-lishes credibility. In Exodus 4:1, Moses is saying, "But behold, they will not believe me or listen to and obey my voice; for they will say, The Lord has not appeared to you." What is he asking for? Credibility. When you have vision, and you know what God has called you to do, that vision establishes credibility.

People will say, "Who do you think you are doing this?"   "Who are you?" Everybody wants credibility, but when you have vision, whether you have the praise of man or not, you know you have credibility with God!

4. ABILITY. Vision establishes abil-ity. Moses had a habit of saying, "I am not! I cannot! Choose someone else!" In Exodus 4:10, Moses says, "O Lord, I am not eloquent or a man of words, neither before nor since You have spoken to Your servant; for I am slow of speech and have

a heavy and awkward tongue." In other words, he was talking about his inability.

BUT, in verse 12, God says, "Now therefore go, and I will be with your mouth and will teach you what you shall say." God always emphasizes the ability! When God gave Moses vision, it established his ability. God-given ability! When you recapture your vision, you also have imparted into you God's divine ability to get the job done!

5. COURAGE. Vision establishes courage. We have been reading in Exodus of all the obstacles Moses faced when God called him to fulfill this vision, his "inability" to perform, to speak, and his age, but God ignored all that and gave Moses courage.

Verse 18 begins, "And Moses went..." What happened? He got the vision! He got the vision of what God wanted him to do, and Moses went. That means vision establishes the courage to do what God told you to do and the courage to go after what God says is yours!

6. BOLDNESS. Vision establishes boldness. Notice in Exodus 5:1, it says, "Afterward Moses and Aaron went in and told Pharaoh, Thus says the Lord, the God of Israel, Let My people go..." When this first started, Moses was saying, "God's people". Now it's "My people!" What happened? Vision established boldness.

This is not the same man who was saying, "I am not...I can't do...I can't talk.." Now he is boldly declaring to Pharaoh, "you let My people go!" The Word says in Philippians 1:14 (Amplified), "And most of the brethren have derived fresh confidence in the Lord because of my chains and are much more BOLD to speak and publish fearlessly the Word of God (acting with more freedom and indifference to the consequences)."

7. PERSEVERANCE. Vision establishes perseverance. Notice the illustration of Moses' tenacity. God instructed him to approach Pharaoh and tell him, "Let My people go!" And Pharaoh would not. Moses said again, "Let My people go!" And Pharaoh would not. He continually went back again and again. What happened? Vision established a NO QUIT attitude! Finally, he won! He seized the dream that God gave him by the perseverance that was established in his life once he recaptured his dream.

Hebrews 12:1 (Amplified) says, "...let us run with patient endurance and steady and active persistence the appointed course of the race that is set before us." We all have a purpose or a calling in life that God expects us to fulfill, but we must have patience and perseverance in order to carry it out.

You have what it takes to be victorious just like Moses! In order to obtain these seven qualities in your life, you must fully RECAPTURE YOUR DREAMS! Go back to the basics of God's Word and allow the Word to stir up the gifts that lie within you. Don't settle for a life with no goals, no vision, and no purpose. You know that God has called YOU for a reason, so go for it! Don't let Satan or anyone else talk you out of it!

Begin reading and studying God's Word, spend time praying and talking with the Lord, and pray in the Holy Spirit - it will produce JOY on the inside of you and will enable you to go after these dreams with anticipation! Fully expect your dreams to be fulfilled! DON'T LET GO OF YOUR DREAMS!

Special Message
from Jerry Savelle...

I believe that after reading this book, you have realized that God has called YOU for a purpose! Remember that when God gives you purpose, He also will make it come to pass, BUT your responsibility is to hold on to the dream! Don't let go! I encourage you to make this your daily confession in order to recapture your dreams and see them fulfilled:

Father, in the Name of Jesus, I, _____, receive Your Word into my spirit on this date, _____. I believe that from this date forward, I will make every effort possible to spend time with You and spend time reading and studying Your Word. I realize that in Your presence is fullness of joy and joy gives me the strength to go after my dreams! I believe that I have the spirit of revival in my heart and a fire burning so bright that it will cause me to go after the calling on my life no matter what obstacle the devil might bring! I will not let go of my dreams! I am holding fast to my dreams; gripping them tightly with force so that nothing and no one can take them from me. I will not let time or people steal my dreams from me in Jesus' Name. Satan, I rebuke you and all your cohorts, and I demand in Jesus' Name, your departure out of my mind, out of my thought life, out of my emotions, and out of my dreams! In Jesus' Name, I recapture my destiny and receive joy in my heart to finish my course! I will not let go of my dreams - I WILL see them fulfilled in Jesus' Name! Amen.

Are you going to heaven?

If you were to die today, are you certain that you would go to Heaven? If you have accepted Jesus Christ as your personal Lord and Savior, you can be assured that when you die, you will go directly into the presence of God in Heaven. If you have not accepted Jesus as your personal Lord and Savior, is there any reason why you can't make Jesus the Lord of your life right now? Please pray this prayer out loud, and as you do, pray with a sincere and trusting heart, and you will be born again.

Dear God in Heaven,

I come to you in the Name of Jesus to receive salvation and eternal life. I believe that Jesus is Your Son. I believe that He died on the cross for my sins, and that You raised Him from the dead. I receive Jesus now into my heart and make Him the Lord of my life. Jesus, come into my heart. I welcome you as my Lord and Savior. Father, I believe Your Word that says I am now saved. I confess with my mouth that I am saved and born again. I am now a child of God.

Dr. Jerry Savelle is a noted author, evangelist, and teacher who travels extensively throughout the United States, Canada and overseas. He is president of Jerry Savelle Ministries International, a ministry of many outreaches devoted to meeting the needs of believers all over the world.

Well-known for his balanced Biblical teaching, Dr. Savelle has conducted seminars, crusades and conventions for over twenty years as well as holding meetings in local churches and fellowships. He is being used to help bridge the gap between the travelling ministry and the local church. In these meetings, he is able to encourage and assist pastors in perfecting the saints for the work of the ministry. He is in great demand today because of his inspiring message of victory and faith and his accurate and entertaining illustrations from the Bible. He teaches the uncompromising Word of God with a power and an authority that is exciting, but with a love that delivers the message directly to the spirit man.

When Dr. Savelle was 12 years old, God spoke to his heart as he was watching the healing ministry of Oral Roberts on television. God told him that He was calling him into the ministry. Some years later, Dr. Savelle made Jesus Christ the Lord of his life and since that time has been moving in the light of that calling.

Dr. Savelle is the founder of Overcoming Faith Churches of Kenya, and the missions outreach of his ministry extends to over 50 different countries around the world. His ministry also delivers the powerful message of God's Word across the United States through the JSM Prison Ministry Outreach.

Dr. Savelle has authored a number of books and has an extensive cassette teaching tape ministry. Thousands of books, tapes, and videos are distributed around the world each year through Jerry Savelle Ministries.